Gold Stars®

Big Workbook
Handwriting

Bath · New York · Cologne · Melbourne · Delhi
Hong Kong · Shenzhen · Singapore

Helping your child

- Remember that the activities in this book should be enjoyed by your child. Try to find a quiet place to work.

- Always give your child lots of encouragement and praise.

- Remember that the gold stars are a reward for effort as well as for achievement.

- Your child does not need to complete each page in one go. Always stop before your child grows tired, and come back to the same page another time.

- It is important to work through the pages in the right order because the activities do get progressively more difficult.

- Gold Stars uses a standard handwriting style. Check with your child's school as some letters, such as 'k' and 'f', may be taught differently.

This edition published by Parragon in 2018

Parragon Books Ltd
Chartist House
15–17 Trim Street
Bath BA1 1HA, UK
www.parragon.com

Copyright © Parragon Books Ltd 2009–2018

Written by Nina Filipek and Catherine Casey
Illustrated by Simon Abbott and Adam Linley
Educational Consultant: Janet Rose

ISBN 978-1-4748-7580-6

Printed in China

Contents

Pencil control

Trace over the dotted lines to practise moving your pencil. Start on the red dot and follow the arrow.

iTdu2oo mTMaTer if I maky

a m stac

Note for parent: Show your child how to hold the pencil correctly. This activity helps children to practise controlling the pencil.

Trace over the dotted lines starting at the red dots.

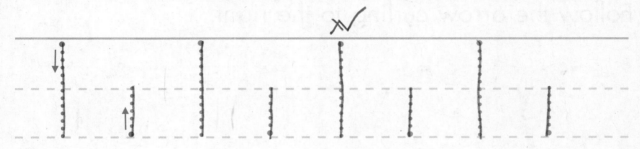

Trace down over the dotted lines to draw the leaves.
Trace up over the dotted lines to draw the grass.

Note for parent: This activity gives your child further practice of up and down lines in preparation for letters such as **r**, **n**, **m**, **h** and **k**.

7

Making clockwise shapes

Trace over the dotted lines starting on the red dot.
Follow the arrow curling to the right.

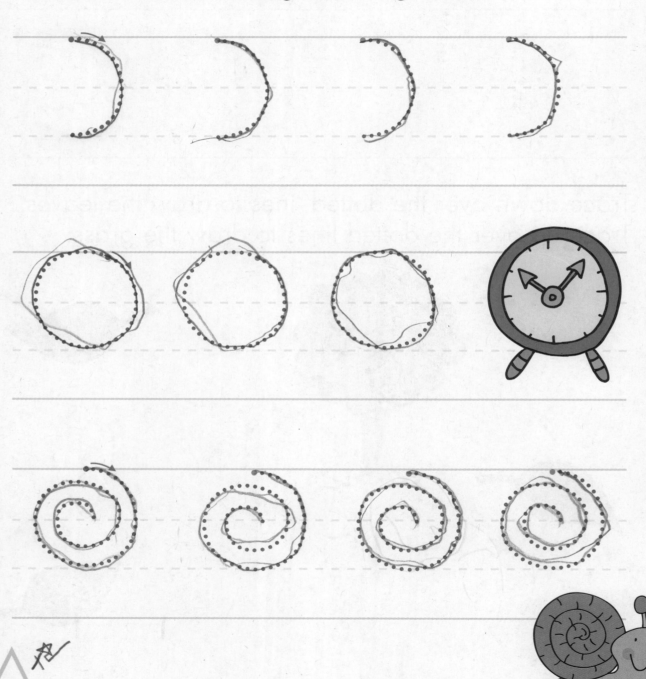

Note for parent: Talk to your child about a clockwise direction. Look at the hands of a clock and point out the way they move around the clock face.

Trace over the dotted lines starting on the red dot.
Colour the picture.

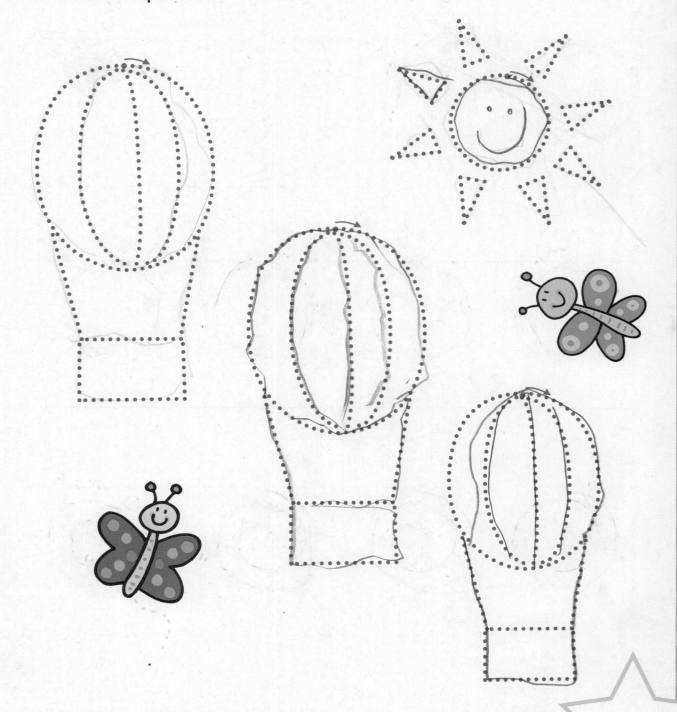

Making anticlockwise shapes

Trace over the dotted lines starting at the top. Follow the arrow curling to the left.

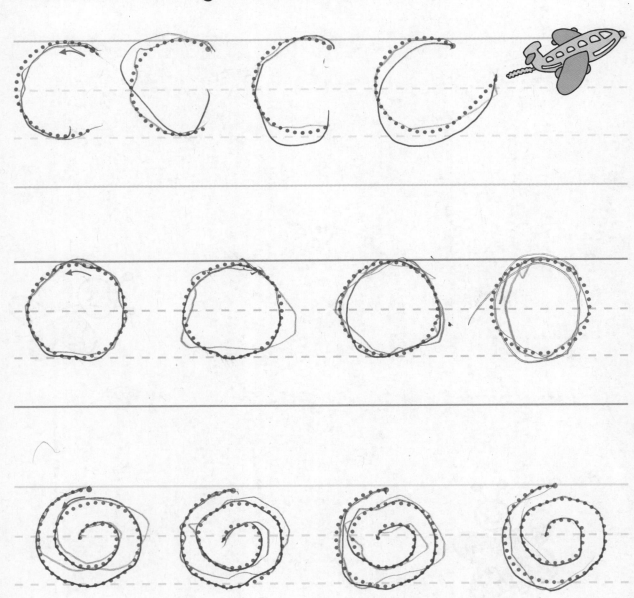

Note for parent: This activity helps children to practise anticlockwise shapes to prepare for writing letters such as **c**, **e**, **a**, **d**, **o** and many more.

Trace over the dotted lines starting on the red dots.
Colour the picture.

Making zigzag shapes

Trace over the dotted lines to draw zigzag shapes.

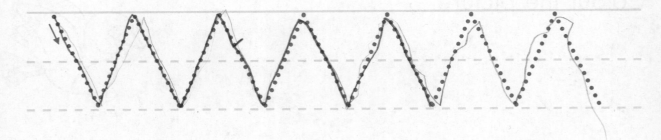

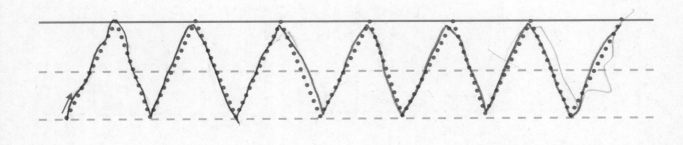

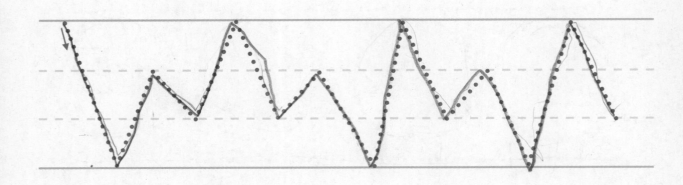

Note for parent: You can help your child improve their fine motor skills and build finger strength by doing activities such as threading or using playdough.

Trace over the dotted lines to draw more zigzag shapes.

Making more shapes

Trace over the shape at the start of each row, then copy the shape to draw some on your own.

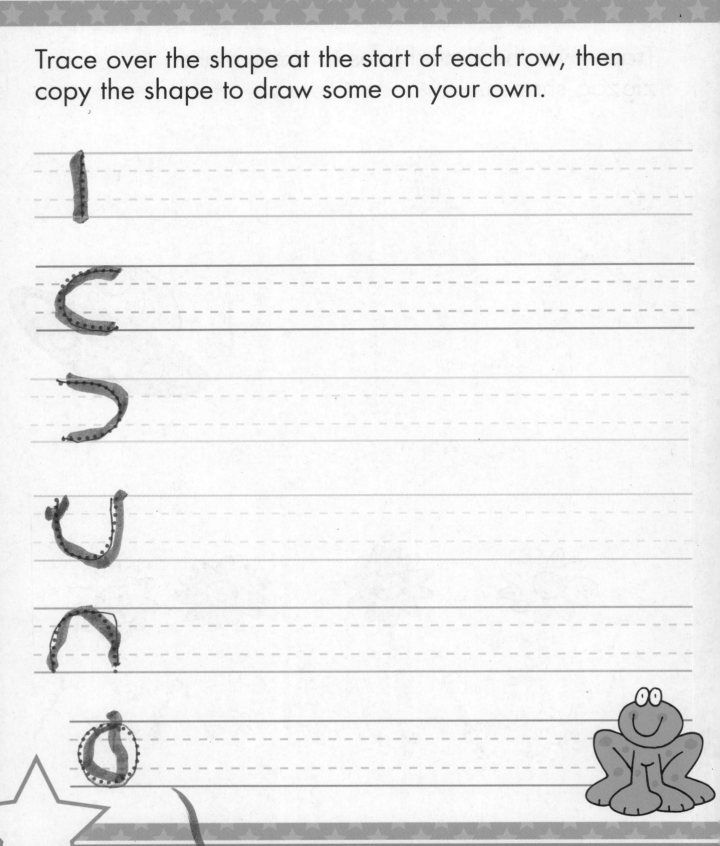

Note for parent: This activity encourages independence and confidence with pencil control by asking children to copy the shapes without tracing.

Trace over the dotted lines to write **l**. The letter **l** starts on the top line, goes down and flicks right at the bottom.

Trace over the letter **l** to finish the words.

ladybird ladybird

 lamb lamb lamb

leaf leaf leaf leaf

Write the letter **l** on your own.

Note for parent: The flick (or serif) is drawn at the bottom of the **l** in preparation for joining to other letters later on.

Writing letter t

Trace over the dotted lines to write **t**. The letter **t** goes down and ends with a flick. Then add a bar across.

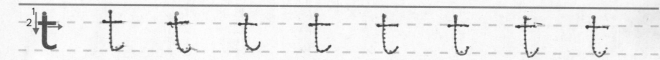

Trace over the letter **t** to finish the words.

tent tent tent tent

train train train

tree tree tree tree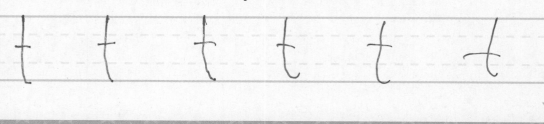

Write the letter **t** on your own.

Note for parent: Notice that lower-case **t** is not as tall as **b**, **d** or the other tall letters.

Writing letter i

Trace over the dotted lines to write **i**. The letter **i** goes down and flicks. Then add a dot above.

i i i i i i i i i i i

Trace over the letter **i** to finish the words.

ice cream ice cream

 igloo igloo igloo

iron iron iron

Write the letter **i** on your own.

Note for parent: The flick (also called a serif) is drawn at the bottom of the **i** in preparation for joining to other letters later on.

Writing letter j

Trace over the lines to write **j**. The letter **j** goes down then curves left. Then add a dot on top.

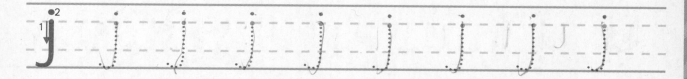

Trace over the letter **j** to finish the words.

jelly jelly jelly jelly

 jug jug jug jug

jigsaw jigsaw

Write the letter **j** on your own.

Note for parent: Notice that the letter **j** is drawn down to the bottom line and curves to the left.

19

Writing letter u

Trace over the dotted lines to write **u**. The letter **u** goes down, around, up and then down again.

u u u u u u u u u

Write the letter **u** to complete the words.

umbrella umbrella

up up up up up

under under under

Write the letter **u** on your own.

u u u u u u u u u u u u u u u u

Note for parent: The letters **u** and **y** are formed in a similar way except that **y** has a tail.

Trace over the dotted lines to write **y**. The letter **y** goes down, around, up and then down below the line with a tail curling left.

y y y y y y y y y

Write the letter **y** to complete the words.

yo-yo yo-yo yo-yo

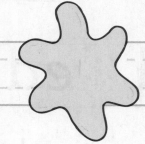 yellow yellow

yum yum yum

Write the letter **y** on your own.

yyyyyyyyyyyyyyyyyyyyyyyyyyyy

Writing letter r

Trace over the dotted lines to write **r**. The letter **r** goes down, then up again and over.

r r r r r r r r r r

Trace over the letter **r** to finish the words.

robot robot robot

 red red red red

ring ring ring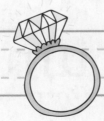

Write the letter **r** on your own.

r r r r r r r r r r r r r r r r r r r r r r r r r r r r r

Note for parent: This activity focuses on the formation of the letters **r** and **n**. You can point out the similarities in how they are formed.

Trace over the dotted lines to write **n**. The letter **n** goes down, then up again, then bends back down.

n n n n n n n n n

Trace over the letter **n** to finish the words.

nest nest nest

net net net net

name name name Oliver

Write the letter **n** on your own.

Writing letter m

Trace over the letter **m**. The letter **m** goes down, up and over, then up and over again.

m m m m m m m m m

Trace over the letter **m** to finish the words.

moon moon moon

 mouse mouse

map map map

Write the letter **m** on your own.

m m m m

Note for parent: The letters **m**, **h** and **k** are formed in a similar way.

Writing letters h and k

Trace over the dotted lines to write **h**. The letter **h** goes down, up halfway, then bends back down.

h h h h h h h h h h

horse horse horse

Write the letter **h** on your own.

h h h

Trace over the letter **k**. It goes down, up halfway, then back round to the line before kicking out.

k k k k k k k k k k

king king king

Write the letter **k** on your own.

k

Writing letter b

Trace over the lines to write **b**. The letter **b** goes down, halfway up then round to join at the bottom.

b b b b b b b b b b

bed bed bed bed

 bee bee bee bee

bell bell bell bell

Write the letter **b** on your own.

b

Note for parent: These two pages focus on the formation of the letters **b** and **p**, their similarities and differences.

Trace over the lines to write **p**. The letter **p** goes down to make a tail then up again, then curves round.

p p p p p p p p p p

Trace over the letter **p** to finish the words.

panda panda

 pen pen pen pen

pear pear pear

Write the letter **p** on your own.

p p p p

Writing letters c and e

Trace over the dotted lines to write **c**. The letter **c** goes down and round.

c c c c c c c c c c c c

car car car ar

Write the letter **c** on your own.

Trace over the dotted lines to write **e**. The letter **e** starts in the middle, curves up and goes halfway round.

e e e e e e e e e e

egg egg egg egg

Write the letter **e** on your own.

Note for parent: Encourage your child to try to make the letters c and e the same size.

Writing letter a

Trace over the dotted lines to write **a**. The letter **a** goes down, around and back down again.

a̅ a a a a a a a a

Trace over the letter **a** to finish the words.

apple apple apple

 ant ant ant ant

arrow arrow arrow

Write the letter **a** on your own.

Note for parent: Show your child how the **a** joins at the top and then comes back down to the line.

29

Writing letter d

Trace over the dotted lines to write **d**. The letter **d** goes down, around, up to the top and then back down.

d d d d d d d d d d d d

Trace over the letter **d** to finish the words.

dog dog dog dog

digger digger

duck duck duck

Write the letter **d** on your own.

Note for parent: Show your child how the letters **a** and **d** are similar.

Trace over the dotted lines to write **o**. The letter **o** goes round to the left and joins up at the start.

ō o o o o o o o o o

Trace over the letter **o** to finish the words.

orange orange

 open open open

owl owl owl owl

Write the letter **o** on your own.

Note for parent: The letters **o**, **a** and **d** are all anticlockwise letters.

31

Writing letter g

Trace over the dotted lines to write **g**. The letter **g** goes down, round, then down with the tail curling left.

 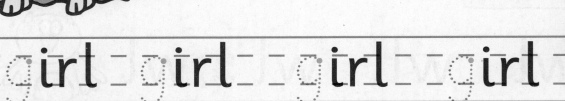

Write the letter **g** on your own.

Note for parent: This activity groups **g** and **q** together because they have a similar formation, except that the tails go in different directions.

Trace over the dotted lines to write **q**. The letter **q** goes round, then down with the tail flicking right.

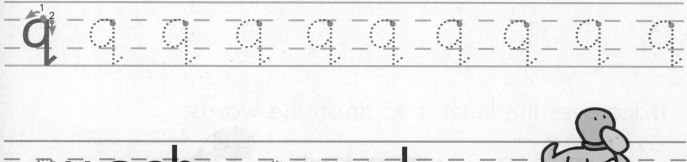

quack   quack

queen   queen

quilt   quilt   quilt

Write the letter **q** on your own.

Writing letter s

Trace over the dotted lines to write **s**. The letter **s** curves backwards then curves forwards.

s s s s s s s s s s s

Trace over the letter **s** to finish the words.

snake snake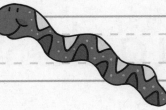

 socks socks socks

sun sun sun sun

Write the letter **s** on your own.

Note for parent: The letter **s** is tricky because it turns both anticlockwise and clockwise.

Trace over the lines to write **f**. The letter **f** curves down to make a tail, then finishes with a bar across.

Trace over the letter **f** to finish the words.

ish fish fish fish

 flower flower

flag flag flag

Write the letter **f** on your own.

Writing letter v

Trace over the dotted lines to write **v**. The letter **v** goes diagonally down then diagonally up, making a sharp point.

v v v v v v v v v v v v v v v

Trace over the letter **v** to finish the words.

van van van van

 vase vase vase

violin violin

Write the letter **v** on your own.

Trace over the dotted lines to write **w**. The letter **w** goes diagonally down, then up, then down, then up again!

w w w w w w w w

Trace over the letter **w** to finish the words.

witch witch

wand wand wand

wall wall wall

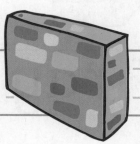

Write the letter **w** on your own.

Writing letter x

Trace over the dotted lines to write **x**. The letter **x** goes diagonally down to the right, then down to the left.

Trace over the letter **x** to finish the words.

fox fox fox fo

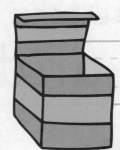 box box box box

x-ray x-ray x-ray

Write the letter **x** on your own.

Note for parent: Discuss with your child how their pencil must be lifted off the page to write **x**.

Writing letter z

Trace over the dotted lines to write **z**. The letter **z** goes across, then down to the left, then across again.

1→ Ž z z z z z z z z z

Trace over the letter **z** to finish the words.

zebra zebra

 zip zip zip zip

buzz buzz buzz

Write the letter **z** on your own.

Note for parent: Compare the letter **z** with the letter **s** on page 34 and talk about the differences.

39

From a to z

Some of the letters are missing from these jars. Write in the missing letters. Follow the order from **a** to **z**.

Trace over the dotted lines to write **2**. The number **2** goes up, round and down, then across to the right.

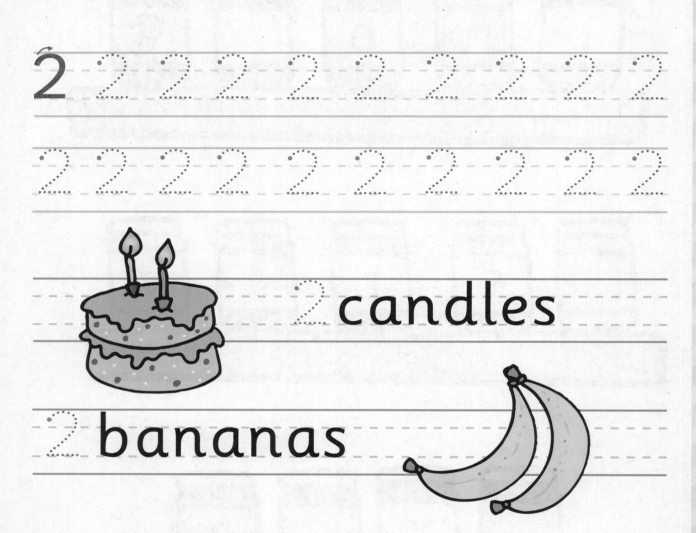

2 candles

2 bananas

Write the number **2** on your own.

Note for parent: This activity groups **2**, **3** and **5** together because they have a similar formation. The pencil moves up and down to form the numbers, ending in different directions.

Writing 3 and 5

Trace over the dotted lines to write **3**. The number **3** curves round to the middle, then round again.

3 cakes

Write the number **3** on your own.

Trace over the dotted lines to write **5**. The number **5** goes down halfway then round, then straight across the top.

5 butterflies

Write the number **5** on your own.

Writing 0 and 6

Trace over the dotted lines to write **0**. The number **0** curves to the left then round again to join at the top.

0 0 0 0 0 0 0 0 0 0

0 to 60

Write the number **0** on your own.

0 0 0 0 0 0 0 0 0 0 0 0 0 0 0 0 0 0 0 0 0 0 0 0 0 0 0 0 0 0 0 0 0 0 0 0 0 0 0 0 0 0 0 0

Trace over the dotted lines to write **6**. The number **6** goes down then round, then joins in the middle.

6 6 6 6 6 6 6 6 6

6 cars

Write the number **6** on your own.

6 6 6 6 6 6 6 6 6 6 6 6 6 6 6 6 6 6 6 6 6 6 6 6 6 6 6 6 6 6 6 6 6 6 6 6 6 6 6

Note for parent: Notice how the number 6 starts on the top line but curls back up to the centre line.

Writing 8 and 9

Trace over the dotted lines to write **8**. The number **8** curves round to the middle, then curves the other way.

8 balloons

Write the number **8** on your own.

Trace over the dotted lines to write **9**. The number **9** goes down halfway, then up to the top and straight down again.

9 balloons

Write the number **9** on your own.

Note for parent: Notice how the number **8** starts in the same way as the letter **s**.

Writing 1 and 4

Trace over the dotted lines to write **1**. The number **1** flicks up and then goes straight down.

1 1 1 1 1 1 1 1 1 1

one 1

Write the number **1** on your own.

Trace over the dotted lines to write **4**. The number **4** goes diagonally down then across. Then draw a line straight down.

4 4 4 4 4 4 4 4 4

four 4

Write the number **4** on your own.

4 4 4 4 4 4 4 4 4

Note for parent: Discuss with your child how, to complete number **4**, the pencil must be lifted off the page.

Writing 7 and 10

Trace over the dotted lines to write **7**. The number **7** goes across then diagonally down.

7 7 7 7 7 7 7 7 7

7 **seven**

7

Write the number **7** on your own.

Trace over the dotted lines to write **10**. The number **10** is made up from **1** and **0**.

10 10 10 10 10 10 10

10 **ten**

10

Write the number **10** on your own.

Note for parent: Show your child how to write the numbers **1** and **0** close together to make **10**.

47

0 **1** **2** **3** **4**

Trace the numbers from 0 to 9, then write each number yourself.

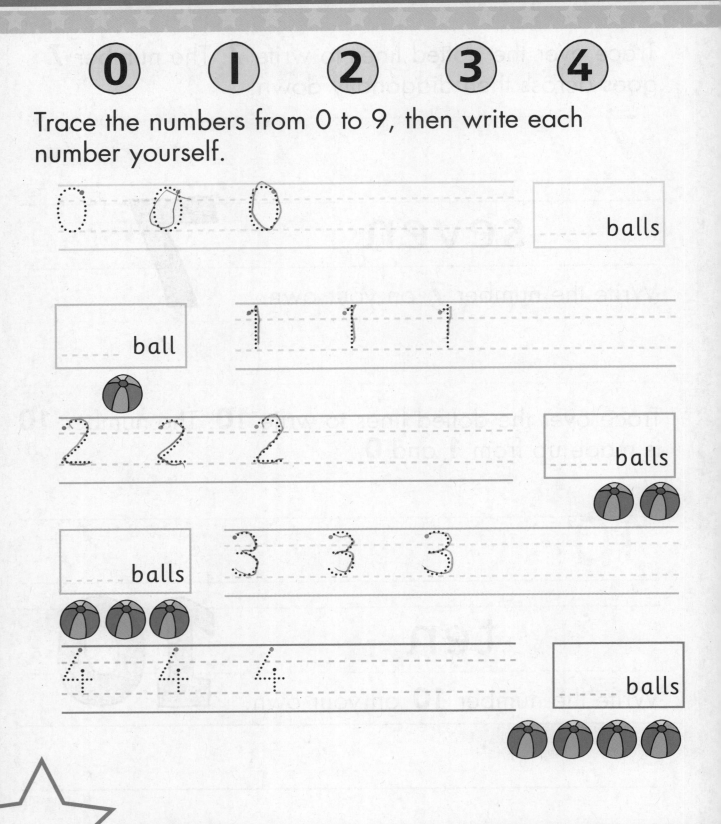

0   0   0

_____ balls

_____ ball

1   1   1

2   2   2

_____ balls

_____ balls

3   3   3

4   4   4

_____ balls

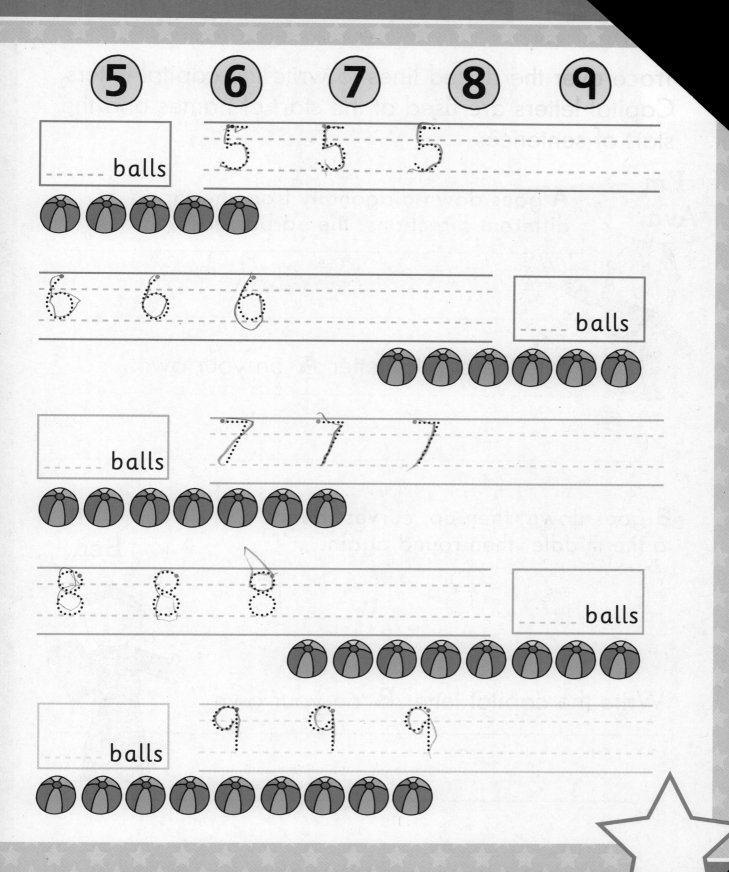

5 6 7 8 9

5 5 5

_____ balls

6 6 6

_____ balls

7 7 7

_____ balls

8 8 8

_____ balls

9 9 9

_____ balls

e dotted lines to write the capital letters.
s are used at the start of names and the
ces.

I'm Ava.

A goes down diagonally from the top in different directions, then a bar goes across.

A A A A A A

Write the capital letter **A** on your own.

B goes down, then up, curves round to the middle, then round again.

B B B B B

I'm Ben.

Write the capital letter **B** on your own.

Note for parent: This activity shows your child how to write and use a capital letter when writing a person's name.

Trace over the dotted lines to write the capital letters.

I'm Cara.

C goes halfway round.

C   C   C   C   C

Write the capital letter **C** on your own.

D goes down, then back to the top, then curves down to the line.

I'm Daisy.

D   D   D   D   D

Write the capital letter **D** on your own.

Trace over the dotted lines to write the capital letters.

I'm Ella.

E goes down first, then across, across, across.

Write the capital letter **E** on your own.

F goes down first, then across, across.

I'm Fin.

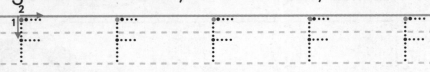

Write the capital letter **F** on your own.

Writing capitals G and H

Trace over the dotted lines to write the capital letters.

I'm George.

G curves round then up halfway to finish with a bar across.

G G G G G

Write the capital letter **G** on your own.

H goes down, down again, then across the middle.

H H H H H H

I'm Harry.

Write the capital letter **H** on your own.

Writing capitals I and J

Trace over the dotted lines to write the capital letters.

I goes down then across top and bottom.

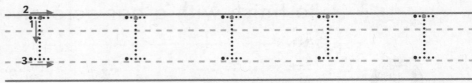

Write the capital letter **I** on your own.

J goes down and curls, then across at the top.

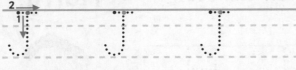

Write the capital letter **J** on your own.

Note for parent: Encourage your child to try to read the names written on the labels.

Trace over the dotted lines to write the capital letters.

K goes down, then diagonally to the middle before kicking out.

K K K K K

Katie

Write the capital letter **K** on your own.

L goes down then across.

L L L L L

Lila

Write the capital letter **L** on your own.

Writing capitals M and N

Capital letters are also used at the beginning of place names. Trace over the dotted lines to write the capital letters.

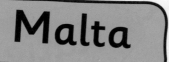

M goes down then up, then diagonally down, diagonally up, then down again.

Write the capital letter **M** on your own.

N goes down then up, then diagonally down, then up again.

Write the capital letter **N** on your own.

Note for parent: This activity reinforces how capital letters are used for place names.

Trace over the dotted lines to write the capital letters.

O goes round anticlockwise.

Oman

O O O O O

Write the capital letter **O** on your own.

P goes down then up, then curves round to the middle.

P P P P P

Poland

Write the capital letter **P** on your own.

Writing capitals Q and R

Trace over the dotted lines to write the capital letters. Then complete the road names.

Q goes round, then finishes with a diagonal bar.

Q   Q   Q   Q   Q

___ueens Drive

Write the capital letter **Q** on your own.

R goes down then up, curves round to the middle then kicks out.

R   R   R   R   R

___egents ___oad

Write the capital letter **R** on your own.

Note for parent: This activity shows your child how to use capital letters for road names.

Dinosaur names begin with capital letters. Trace over the dotted lines to write the capital letters. Then complete the dinosaur names.

S curves backwards then curves forwards.

S S S S S

___tegosaurus

Write the capital letter **S** on your own.

T goes down then across the top.

T T T T

___elmatosaurus

Write the capital letter **T** on your own.

Note for parent: Encourage your child to try reading the dinosaur names.

59

Trace over the dotted lines to write the capital letters. Then complete the dinosaur names.

U goes down then up.

U U U U

___ltrasaurus

Write the capital letter **U** on your own.

V goes diagonally down then up.

V V V V

Draw your own dinosaur here and give it a name beginning with **V**.

Write the capital letter **V** on your own.

Writing capitals W and X

Trace over the dotted lines to write the capital letters.
Then write capital letters to complete the signs.

W goes diagonally down then diagonally
up (twice)!

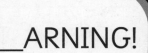

__ARNING!

Write the capital letter **W** on your own.

NO
E__IT

X goes diagonally down in
different directions.

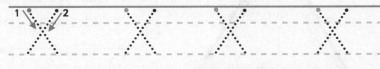

Write the capital letter **X** on your own.

Note for parent: Remind your child that the pencil is lifted to complete the letter **X**.

61

Writing capitals Y and Z

Trace over the dotted lines to write the capital letters. Then write capital letters to complete the signs.

Y goes diagonally down to the middle, then diagonally down the other way.

GIVE
WA__

Y Y Y Y

Write the capital letter **Y** on your own.

DANGER
__ONE

Z goes across, then diagonally down, then across again.

Z Z Z Z

Write the capital letter **Z** on your own.

Note for parent: Capital **Y** and **Z** are double the height of a lower-case letter.
Use the line at the top as a guide.

Joining double ee

Trace and copy the letters keeping your pencil on the page. Draw joined loops for double *ee*.

ee *ee*

Write *ee* to complete these words.

b*ee*

tr*ee*

thr*ee*

Write *ee* in the middle to complete these words.

gr*ee*n

sh*ee*p

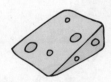

ch*ee*se

Note for parent: The two *e* letters should be the same height.

63

Joining *e* and *a*

Trace and copy the letters keeping your pencil on the page. Go round to join to *a*.

ea *ea*

Write *ea* to complete these words. Then copy the words in full.

ear

read

bear

pear

leaf

Note for parent: The dashed line provides a guide for the height of the lower-case letters.

Joining c and e

Trace and copy the letters keeping your pencil on the page. Go up in a loop to join to *e*.

ce   ce

Write *ce* to complete these words. Then copy the words in full. Capital letters do not join.

dice

mice

face

space

December

Joining e and d

Trace and copy the letters keeping your pencil on the page. Go round to join to *d* in the middle.

ed ed

Write *ed* to complete these words.

 r_ed  b_ed  f_ed  l_ed

Write *ed* to change these words to something that happened in the past.

 walk   jump

 play    clean

Joining *a* and *i*

Trace and copy the letters keeping your pencil on the page. Go up to join to *i* at the top.

ai   *ai*

Write *ai* to complete these words. Then copy the words in full.

rain

chain

chair

snail

train

Note for parent: This activity introduces a common vowel join.

Joining double oo

Trace and copy the letters keeping your pencil on the page. Join to the second o with a bar at the top.

oo oo

Write oo to complete these words. Then copy the words in full.

 spoon

 door

 hook

 wood

 book

Note for parent: This activity will help your child to practise forming the bar join.

Joining o and w

Trace and copy the letters keeping your pencil on the page. Join to *w* with a bar at the top.

ow ow

Write *ow* to complete these words.

cow   grow   snow   throw

Write *ow* to begin the song.

R   r   r

your boat!

Note for parent: This activity will help your child to practise forming letters of a consistent shape and size.

Trace and copy the letters keeping your pencil on the page. Join to *u* with a bar at the top.

ou *ou*

Write *ou* to complete these words. Then copy the words in full.

 house

 *cloud*

 four

 round

 mouth

Note for parent: Encourage your child to form each letter carefully and not to rush through the activities.

Joining *ch* and *ck*

Trace and copy the letters keeping your pencil on the page. Go up to join *h* and *k* at the top.

ch *ch*

ck *ck*

Write *ck* and *ch* to complete these words.

clo*ck*

wat*ch*

Write *ch* to add these items to the shopping basket.

erries

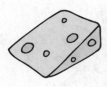

eese

ocolate

Joining double _tt_

Trace and copy the letters keeping your pencil on the page. Go up to join to the next _t_ at the top. Draw a bar across both letters.

_tt_ _tt_

Write _tt_ to complete these words.

 ki**tt**en

 bu**tt**er

  mi**tt**en

  bu**tt**on

Add _t_ or _tt_ to complete the weather chart.

ho**tt** ho**tt**er ho**tt**est

 Saturday

 Sunday

 Monday

Note for parent: Remember to praise your child for good letter formation.

Joining *t* and *h*

Trace and copy the letters keeping your pencil on the page. Go up to join to *h*. Remember capital letters don't join.

th *th*

Write *th* at the end of the words to make new words.

4th four*th*   **5th** fif*th*

7th seven*th*   **10th** ten*th*

Write *th* to complete the children's names.

 E___ an    Na___ an

 Be___    Saman___ a

Joining double *mm*

Trace and copy the letters keeping your pencil on the page. Go up to join to the next *m* at the top.

mm *mm*

Write *mm* to complete these words.

 mu**mm**y

 su**mm**er

 dru**mm**er

 swi**mm**er

Write *mm* to complete these action words. Which word describes what the girl is doing?

swi ing

hu ing

dru ing

stru ing

Joining double *pp*

Trace and copy the letters keeping your pencil on the page. Go up to join to the next *p* at the top.

pp *pp*

Write *pp* to complete these words.

 a__ple

 pu__y

 pu__et

 fli__er

Write *pp* in the middle of these words to make action words. Which word describes what the people in the picture are doing?

cla__ing

ho__ing

ski__ing

sho__ing

Note for parent: This activity will help your child to practise writing letters that go below the line.

75

Joining e and r

Trace and copy the letters keeping your pencil on the page. Go up to join to *r* at the top.

er *er*

Write *er* to complete these words.

 moth*er*

 broth*er*

 fath*er*

 sist*er*

Write *er* at the end of these words to make new words.

 farm

 sing

 football

 teach

Note for parent: This activity introduces a common word ending.

Joining *b* and *r*

Trace and copy the letters keeping your pencil on the page. Go up to join to the *r* at the top.

br　br

Write *br* to begin these words. Then copy the words in full.

 br**ick**

 br**ead**

 br**anch**

 br**oom**

 br**idge**

Note for parent: This activity introduces a common letter combination.

77

Joining *j* and *u*

Trace and copy the letters keeping your pencil on the page. Go up to join to *u* with a loop.

Write *ju* to begin these words.

 *ju*g

 *ju*mper

 *ju*ngle

 *ju*ice

Can you guess what the clown is doing? Write *ju* where it is missing in these words. Were you right?

ggling in the ngle

Note for parent: Good pencil control is needed here so that the loop on the *j* doesn't become too long.

Joining double *ss*

Trace and copy the letters keeping your pencil on the page. Go up to join to the second *s* at the top.

ss *ss*

Write *ss* to finish these words. Then copy the words in full.

gra*ss*

dre*ss*

cro*ss*

gla*ss*

hi*ss*

Note for parent: These letters can be tricky but practice will help your child gain confidence.

Joining a and y

Trace and copy the letters keeping your pencil on the page. Go up to join to y at the top.

ay *ay*

Write *ay* to finish these words. Then copy the words in full. Remember capital letters don't join.

 play

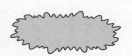 hay

 birthday

 holiday

 Monday

Note for parent: For extra *a* and *y* practice, ask your child to write the other days of the week.

Joining *l* and *y*

Trace and copy the letters keeping your pencil on the page. Go up to join to *y* at the top. Remember capital letters don't join.

ly *ly*

Write *ly* to complete these words.

 f*ly*

 Ju*ly*

2×2 multip*ly*

 Yes, please!   rep*ly*

Write *ly* at the end of these words to make new words.

slow   quick

neat   careful

Joining d, g and e

Trace and copy the letters keeping your pencil on the page. Go round to join to g then loop to join to e.

dge dge

Write **dge** to complete these words.

 we*dge*

 ba*dge*

 bri*dge*

 fu*dge*

Write **dge** to complete these words.

 splo

 le

 porri

 he

Note for parent: This activity introduces a common letter combination.

Trace and copy the letters keeping your pencil on the page. Go up to join to *n* at the top. Then *n* goes round to join to *g*.

ing ing

Write *ing* to complete these words.

 k*ing*

 w*ing*

 r*ing*

 s*ing*

Write *ing* at the end of these words to make another word.

 paint

 jump

 fish

 read

Note for parent: This activity will help your child to practise writing a common word ending.

83

Joining double *ff*

Trace and copy the letters. Join the first *f* to the second *f* with a bar.

ff *ff*

Write *ff* to complete these words.

 co*ff*ee

 mu*ff*in

 cu*ff*

 earmu*ff*

Copy the words. The capital letters beginning each word do not join.

Fluffy

Scruffy

Note for parent: Point out that each name begins with a capital letter that is not joined to the lower-case letters.

Trace and copy the letters keeping your pencil on the page. Join to *r* with a bar.

fr   *fr*

Write *fr* to begin these words. Then copy the words in full.

*fr*og

*fr*iend

*fr*uit

*fr*action

*fr*ame

Note for parent: This activity introduces a common letter combination.

85

Joining q and u

Trace and copy the letters keeping your pencil on the page. Go up to join to u at the top.

qu qu

Write *qu* to complete these words.

queen

quilt

2+4=6 equals

square

Write *qu* to complete these words. Then copy the words in full.

quack

squeak

Note for parent: Make your child aware that the letters q and u almost always appear together in the English language.

Joining v and e

Trace and copy the letters keeping your pencil on the page. Join to *e* with a bar at the top.

ve   *ve*

Write *ve* to complete these words. Then copy the words in full.

5	*five*
7	*seven*
11	*eleven*
12	*twelve*
17	*seventeen*

Note for parent: This activity will help your child to practise writing numbers with fluency and accuracy.

87

Joining x and z

Trace and copy the letters *o* and *x* keeping your pencil on the page. Join to *x* with a bar at the top.

ox

Write *ox* to complete these words. Then copy the words in full.

fox

box

We don't join *z* to the other letters. We leave it unjoined. Trace and copy the letters separately.

z z

Write *zz* to complete these words.

pizza

buzz

fizz

Note for parent: It is difficult to join to the letters x and z. In some school handwriting schemes both letters are left unjoined.

Joining s and t

Trace and copy the letters. Start with the *s* and go up to join to the top of the *t*.

st   *st*

Write *st* at the beginning of these words.

 *st***amp**

 *st***ing**

 *st***ring**

 *st***rong**

 START   *st***art**

 STOP   *st***op**

Write the letters *st* on your own.

Note for parent: This activity helps your child to practise joining the common letter string *st*.

89

Joining *t, c* and *h*

Trace and copy the letters. Start with the *t*, go round to join to the top of *c* and then up to the top of *h*.

tch   *tch*

Write *tch* at the end of these words.

witch

hutch

catch

stitch

watch

patch

Write the letters *tch* on your own.

Note for parent: Remind your child to keep the pencil on the page to join the common letter string *tch*.

Joining *i, g* and *h*

Trace and copy the letters *i, g* and *h*. Make a loop to join *g* with *h*.

igh *igh*

Write *igh* to complete these words.

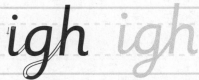 h*igh*

t*ight*

l*ight*

n*ight*

Write *igh* to complete these words. Then copy the words in full.

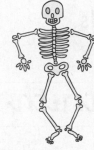

kn*ight*

fr*ight*

Note for parent: This activity helps your child to practise joining the common letter string *igh*.

91

Joining *f, u* and *l*

Trace and copy the letters. Join *f* to *u* with a bar.

ful   *ful*

Write *ful* to complete these words.

 help*ful*

 care*ful*

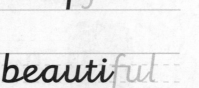 beauti*ful*

 play*ful*

Write *ful* at the end of these words to make new words.

 truth*ful*

 use*ful*

 cheer*ful*

 hope*ful*

Note for parent: This activity introduces the common suffix *ful*.

Joining l, e, s and s

Trace and copy the letters, keeping your pencil on the page.

less *less*

Write *less* to complete these words.

 help*less*

 care*less*

 fear*less*

 rest*less*

Write *less* at the end of these words to make new words.

 end*less*

 use*less*

 harm*less*

 hope*less*

Note for parent: Your child may need to go back to page 79 to remember how to write double *ss*.

93

Joining *i, b, l* and *e*

Trace and copy the letters. Start with the *i*, go up to join *b*, curve up to join *l* and then loop to finish *e*.

ible *ible*

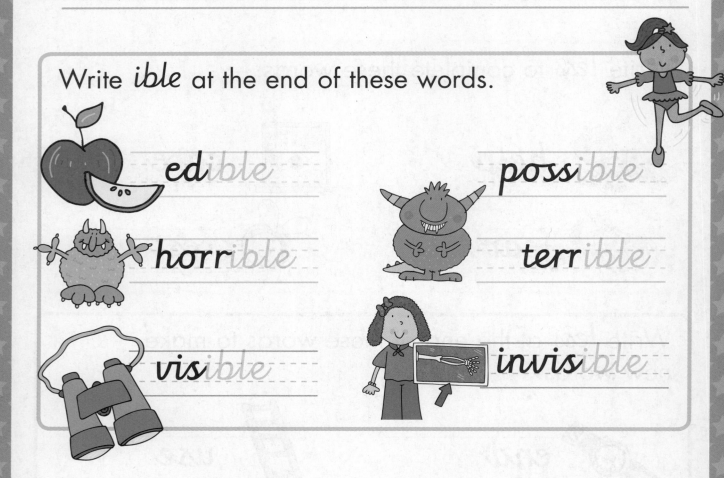

Write *ible* at the end of these words.

edible

horrible

visible

possible

terrible

invisible

Write the letters *ible* on your own.

Note for parent: This activity introduces the common suffix *ible*.

Joining *a, b, l* and *e*

Trace and copy the letters. Start with the *a*, go up to join *b*, curve up to join *l* and then loop to finish *e*.

able　*able*

Write *able* at the end of these words.

table

*c*able

*f*able

*inflat*able

*break*able

*ador*able

Write the letters *able* on your own.

Writing *the* and *and*

Trace the words *the* and *and*. Then copy the words in full. Space the words evenly.

at the park

on the mat

up and down

salt and pepper

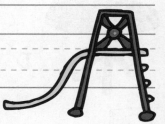

Write the words *the* and *and* on your own.

Note for parent: This activity helps your child practise the common high frequency words *the* and *and*.

Writing *to* and *at*

Trace the words *to* and *at*. Then copy the words.
Space the words evenly.

to **the moon**

to **school**

at **the circus**

at **the shops**

Write the words *to* and *at* on your own.

Note for parent: As well as practising high frequency words, help your child leave even spaces between each word.

97

Writing *in*, *is* and *it*

Trace the words. Then practise writing the word.

in *in*

is *is*

it *it*

Trace over the words *in*, *is* and *it*. Then write the sentence. Remember to leave a space between each word.

Often, *it is* cold *in* Winter.

Usually, *in* Summer *it is* sunny.

Note for parent: This activity helps your child practise writing simple high frequency words in a sentence.

Writing of, go and no

Trace the word. Then practise writing the word.

of of

go go

no no

Trace over the words *of*, *go* and *no*. Then write the sentence. Remember that a sentence starts with a capital letter.

Lots of us go swimming.

He said, no he cannot go.

Note for parent: Look back at page 50 to review capital letters. Explain that capital letters come at the beginning of a sentence.

99

Writing *was* and *his*

Trace the words. Then practise writing them in full.

was *was*

his *his*

Trace over the words *was* and *his* to finish each sentence. Then copy each sentence in full.

The grass *was* green.

 The sky *was* blue.

He put on *his* shoes and *his* socks.

Note for parent: Help your child to practise joining the high frequency words *was* and *his*.

Writing *he*, *she* and *her*

Trace the words. Then practise writing the words.

he he

she she

her her

Trace over the words *he*, *she* and *her*. Then write the sentence. Remember that a sentence starts with a capital letter.

When he went down the slide,

she said her brother was faster.

Note for parent: Practising high frequency words will help your child to write fluently.

101

Writing *for* and can

Trace the words. Then practise writing the words.

for *for*

can can

Trace over the words *for* and *can*. Then copy the sentence.

It is *for* my brother.

I practised *for* the concert.

Please can I go now?

Note for parent: This activity helps your child to practise writing high frequency words in a sentence.

Writing be, we, me and my

Trace the words. Then practise writing the words.

be be

we we

me me

my my

Trace over the words *be, we, me* and *my*. Then write the sentence in full.

If me and my sister go, we will

be good.

Writing *not* and *but*

Trace the words. Then practise writing the words.

not not

but but

Trace over the words *not* and *but*. Then copy the sentence.

It is messy, but it is fun.

It is not your turn.

Oh, but it is not fair.

Writing *all, are* and *had*

Trace the words. Then practise writing the words.

all *all*

are *are*

had *had*

Trace over the words *all, are* and *had*. Then write the sentence. Remember that a sentence starts with a capital letter.

We *are all* going to the beach.

We *all had* to wait for a bus.

Trace the words. Then practise writing the words.

this *this*

have *have*

Trace over the words *this* and *have*. Then copy the sentence.

Now *this* is ready.

You can *have* a cake.

Oh, *this* is scary, but I'll *have* a go.

Writing *that* and *than*

Trace the words. Then practise writing the words.

that *that*

than *than*

Trace over the words *that* and *than*. Then copy the sentence.

Look, *that* spider is big.

It is bigger *than* a penny.

But *that* is smaller *than* this one.

Note for parent: Practising high frequency words helps your child to write more fluently.

107

Writing *they* and *there*

Trace the words. Then practise writing the words.

they *they*

there *there*

Trace over the words *they* and *there*. Then copy the sentence.

Are they in there?

Yes, they are there in the box.

Oh yes, there they are.

Note for parent: Remind your child that capital letters are used at the beginning of a sentence.

Writing *so*, *some* and *said*

Trace the words. Then practise writing the words.

so *so*

some *some*

said *said*

Trace over the words *so*, *some* and *said*. Then write the sentence. Remember that a sentence starts with a capital letter.

She *said* we can have *some*.

Yes, she *said so*.

Note for parent: Practice in writing high frequency words will help your child remember how to spell the words.

109

Writing *you* and *your*

Trace the words. Then practise writing the words.

you *you*

your *your*

Trace over the words *you* and *your*. Then copy the sentence.

Have *you* found *your* toys?

Yes, *you* can play with them too.

I like *your* toys best.

Note for parent: Look back at page 70 to remind your child how to join **o** and **u**.

Writing *on*, *one*, *our* and *out*

Trace the words. Then practise writing the words.

on *on*

one *one*

our *our*

out *out*

Trace over the words *on*, *one*, *our* and *out*. Then copy the sentence.

We are on our way out to get one.

Writing *them* and *then*

Trace the words. Then practise writing the words.

them them

then then

Trace over the words *them* and *then*. Then copy the sentence.

We saw them at the park.

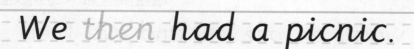

We then had a picnic.

We hugged them, then went home.

Note for parent: Look back to page 73 to remind your child how to joing *th*.

Writing were and where

Trace the words. Then practise writing the words.

were *were*

where *where*

Trace over the words *were* and *where*. Then copy
the sentence.

Yoo-hoo, *where* are you?

Hello, *where were* you?

I thought you *were* hiding.

Note for parent: Discuss with your child how a question mark ? changes the sentence.

113

Writing *what* and *went*

Trace the words. Then practise writing the words.

what *what*

went *went*

Trace over the words *what* and *went*. Then copy the sentence.

We *went* to the zoo.

Tell me *what* you saw.

A monkey that *went*, Oo-oo!

Note for parent: Practice in writing high frequency words will help your child remember how to spell the words.

Writing *like* and *little*

Trace the words. Then practise writing the words.

like   *like*

little   *little*

Trace over the words *like* and *little*. Then copy the sentence.

I *like* cats.

You *like* *little* dogs.

We *like* cats and *little* dogs.

Note for parent: It is usually OK to write a single stroke to cross double *tt*.

Colours

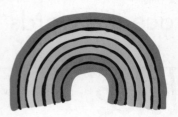

Write the colour words.
First trace them, then copy them.

red red _____

orange orange _____

  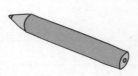 

yellow yellow _____

Note for parent: Colour words are useful high frequency words.

blue   *blue*   -----------------------------

green   *green*   -

black   *black*   -

white   *white*   -

Days of the week

Days of the week start with a capital letter. Trace over the days of the week. Then copy them on the line below.

Monday   Monday

- -

Tuesday   Tuesday

- -

Wednesday   Wednesday

- -

118

Thursday Thursday

Friday Friday

Saturday Saturday

Sunday Sunday

Which is your favourite day?

Months of the year

Months of the year also begin with a capital letter.
Trace over the months of the year.
Then copy them.

January January

February February

March March

April April

May May

June June

Note for parent: This activity focuses on the importance of writing capital letters at the start of the months of the year.

July July

August August

September September

October October

November November

December December

When is your birthday? ----------

These names have been written without capital letters. Rewrite the names on the gift tags using a capital letter to begin each one.

olivia   **sam**   **jack**   **amelia**

Note for parent: Remind your child that capital **O** and **S** are formed in the same way as the lower-case letters, but they are bigger.

Writing an address

Trace the address on the envelope. Then make up an address of your own on the envelope below.

Mr Pinky Bubbledown

3 Toadstool Row

Fern Dale

Meadowville

....

....

....

....

....

Note for parent: This activity gives your child practice in using capital letters in addresses.

123

Letters that don't always join

The letters *b*, *g*, *j* and *p* can be tricky to join so it is sometimes quicker and neater not to join them.

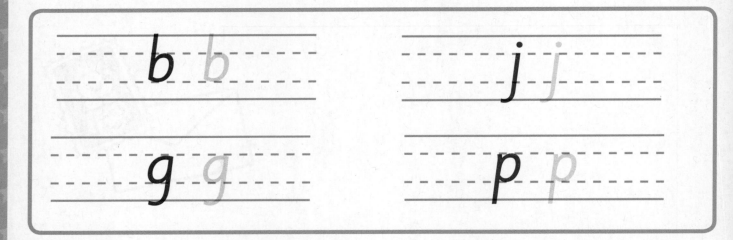

Practise writing these words with letters that don't join.

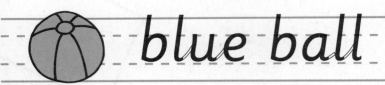
blue ball

green grass

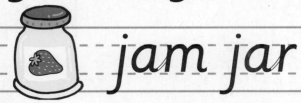
jam jar

pen pal

Note for parent: Ensure the gap between the letters that don't join and the rest of the word is not too big.

The letters x, y, z and s can also be tricky to join, so it is sometimes quicker and neater not to join them.

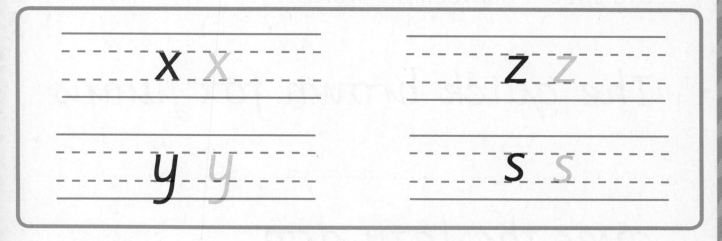

x x   z z

y y   s s

Practise writing these words with letters that don't join.

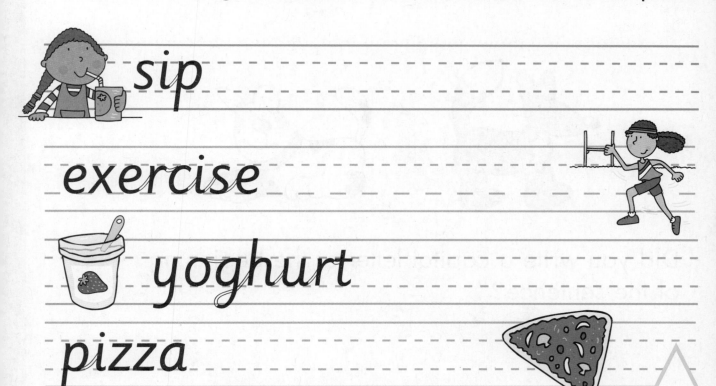

sip

exercise

yoghurt

pizza

Note for parent: Remind your child that capital letters are also not joined.

Copying a sentence

This sentence uses all the letters of the alphabet.
Trace and copy it in your best handwriting.
Leave spaces between the words.

The quick brown fox jumps

....

over the lazy dog.

....

Did you write a capital letter at the beginning
of the sentence?

Note for parent: This activity provides useful revision in the formation of all
the letters of the alphabet.

Copying a poem

Copy out this poem, line by line, in your best handwriting.

If all the world was paper,

....

And all the sea was ink,

....

And all the trees were bread and cheese,

....

What would we have to drink?

....

Write a poster

Trace the words on this poster.

CLASS 1
_____

FANCY DRESS
PARTY
WITH LOTS OF
MUSIC, GAMES
AND FUN!

Write your own
party poster here.

....
....
....
....
....
....